CLINICAL MANUAL

PDMT SCALE, EXERCISES AND INTERVENTIONS

Georgi Distefano, LCSW & Melinda Hohman, Ph.D.

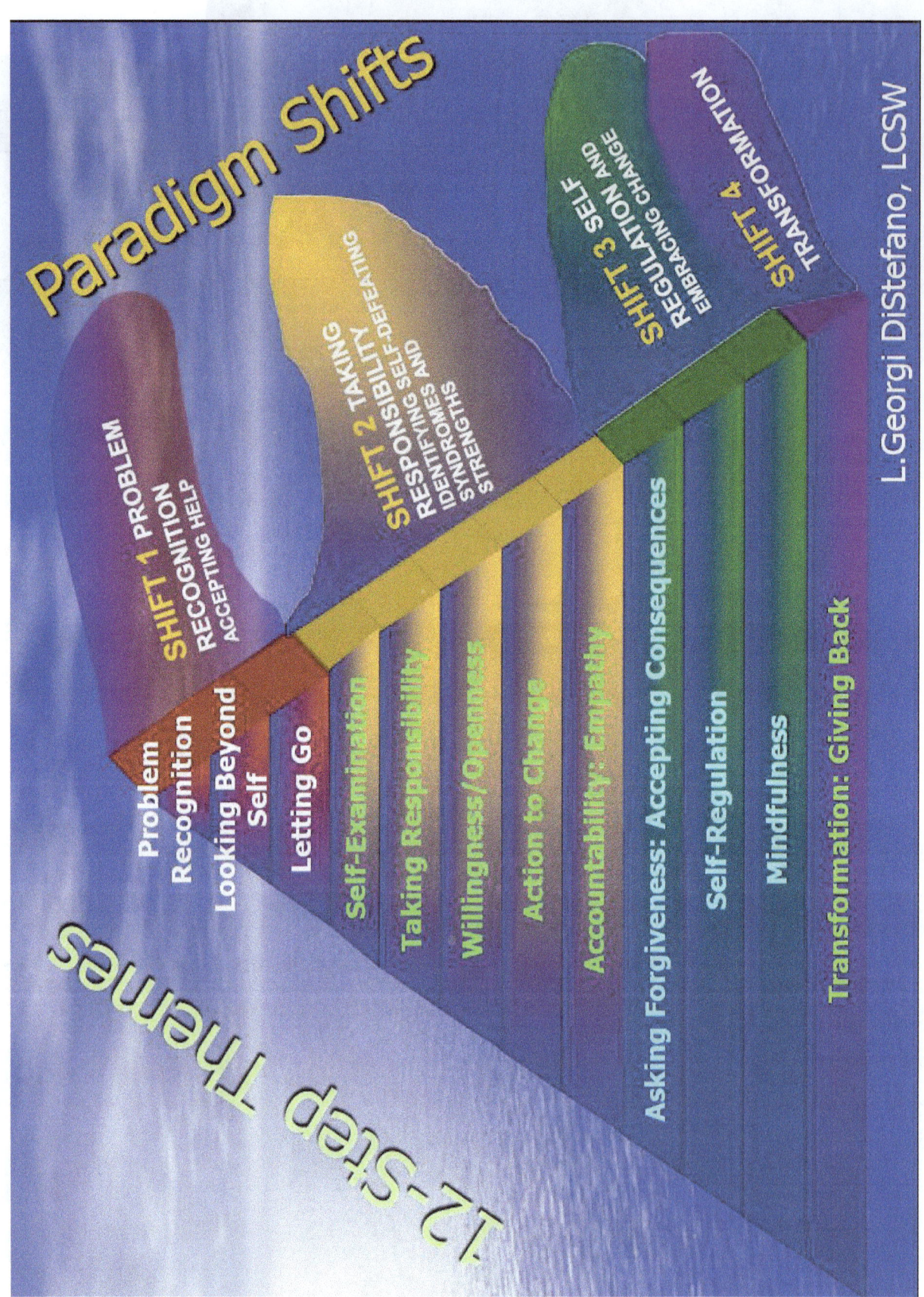

Georgi Distefano, LCSW & Melinda Hohman, Ph.D.

Paradigm Developmental Model of Treatment Scale
Georgi DiStefano, LCSW and Melinda Hohman, PH.D.

Please answer each question as it applies to you right now, using the following scale:

1=Strongly Disagree 2= Disagree 3= Not sure 4=Agree 5=Strongly Agree

1. When I drink/use drugs, I frequently am unable to manage my use   1 2 3 4 5
2. I now believe I have a problem with alcohol/drugs   1 2 3 4 5
3. I realize I need help with my alcohol/drug problem   1 2 3 4 5
4. I now believe that I am an alcoholic/drug addict   1 2 3 4 5
5. I have decided to quit drinking or doing drugs   1 2 3 4 5
6. I am currently attempting abstinence   1 2 3 4 5 _____

7. I understand the characteristics about myself that get me in trouble   1 2 3 4 5
8. I know what my high risk behaviors are   1 2 3 4 5 _____

9. I know what my strengths are that support recovery   1 2 3 4 5
10. I monitor my thoughts and feelings on a daily basis   1 2 3 4 5
11. I manage my self-defeating behaviors regularly   1 2 3 4 5
12. I take a personal inventory regularly and admit mistakes promptly   1 2 3 4 5 _____

13. I am a totally different person now from when I was drinking/using   1 2 3 4 5
14. I have incorporated healthy and productive behaviors into my life   1 2 3 4 5
15. I go to self-help meetings such as AA   1 2 3 4 5 _____

Client's name: _____   Date: _____

Paradigm: _____   Scale Category: _____

Georgi Distefano, LCSW & Melinda Hohman, Ph.D.

PARADIGM SCALE CATEGORIES
Georgi DiStefano, LCSW and Melinda Hohman, Ph.D.

Paradigm I: **Disinterested**

Client is disinterested in addressing alcohol and other drug issues with behavioral change

---

Paradigm I: **Contemplating/Open**

Client is not sure there is a significant alcohol or other drug problem but is open toward exploration of the issue.
Clients are usually non-abstinent but can occasionally be abstinent.

Paradigm II: **Accepting/Implementing**

Client accepts they have an alcohol or other drug problem and is preparing to make behavioral changes or has initiated some behavioral change. Must be abstinent from alcohol and other drugs.

Paradigm II: **Overconfident**

Client has initiated abstinence from alcohol and drug use but is overconfident or unrealistic about the recovery process or is self-managing abstinence.

Paradigm III: **Consistent Action - Sefl-Regulation**

Client is engaged in an active recovery process and action is taken on a consistent basis to manage alcohol, drug and other issues.

Paradigm IV: **Transformation**

Client has fully integrated their recovery process over a significant period of time.

Scoring the PDMT Scale
Georgi DiStefano, LCSW and Melinda Hohman, Ph.D.

	PARADIGM			
	I Problem Recognition	II Taking Responsibility	III Self Regulation	IV Transformation
	Disinterested / Contemplating Abstinent/Non-abstinent (Harm Reduction)	**Accepting Implementing	Consistent Action	Transformation Or ***Overconfident
Q 1-6	≤12 / >12	≥24	≥24	≥24
Q 7-8	Stop / Stop	≥8	≥8	≥8
Q 9-12		<16	16	>16
Q 13-15		stop	12	>12
		MUST BE ABSTINENT FROM ALCOHOL AND OTHER DRUGS		

(Questions column on left: Q 1-6, Q 7-8, Q 9-12, Q 13-15)

Note:
** To move into Paradigm II, score must be 24 or greater AND the answer for question 6 must be agree/strongly agree
*** Overconfident clients (Paradigm II) can often mimic the score of Paradigm IV. Further clinical assessment is required

PRACTICE SCALES

CASE 1

Paradigm Developmental Model of Treatment Scale
Georgi DiStefano, LCSW and Melinda Hohman, Ph.D.

Please answer each question as it applies to you right now, using the following scale:
1=Strongly Disagree   2= Disagree   3= Not sure   4=Agree   5=Strongly Agree

1. When I drink/use drugs, I frequently am unable to manage my use   1 2 3 (4) 5
2. I now believe I have a problem with alcohol/drugs   1 2 3 (4) 5
3. I realize I need help with my alcohol/drug problem   1 2 3 (4) 5
4. I now believe that I am an alcoholic/drug addict   1 2 3 (4) 5
5. I have decided to quit drinking or doing drugs   1 2 3 (4) 5
6. I am currently attempting abstinence   1 2 3 (4) 5   **24**

7. I understand the characteristics about myself that get me in trouble   1 2 3 (4) 5
8. I know what my high risk behaviors are   1 2 3 (4) 5   **8**
9. I know what my strengths are that support recovery   1 2 3 (4) 5
10. I monitor my thoughts and feelings on a daily basis   1 2 (3) 4 5
11. I manage my self-defeating behaviors regularly   1 2 3 (4) 5
12. I take a personal inventory regularly and admit mistakes promptly   1 2 (3) 4 5   **14**

13. I am a totally different person now from when I was drinking/using   1 2 (3) 4 5
14. I have incorporated healthy and productive behaviors into my life   1 2 3 (4) 5
15. I go to self-help meetings such as AA   1 2 3 (4) 5   **11**

Client's name: _____   Date: _____

Paradigm: _____   Scale Category: _____

Georgi Distefano, LCSW & Melinda Hohman, Ph.D.

CASE 2
Paradigm Developmental Model of Treatment Scale
Georgi DiStefano, LCSW and Melinda Hohman, Ph.D.

Please answer each question as it applies to you right now, using the following scale:

| 1=Strongly Disagree | 2= Disagree | 3= Not sure | 4=Agree | 5=Strongly Agree |

1. When I drink/use drugs, I frequently am unable to manage my use   1 (2) 3 4 5
2. I now believe I have a problem with alcohol/drugs   1 (2) 3 4 5
3. I realize I need help with my alcohol/drug problem   1 (2) 3 4 5
4. I now believe that I am an alcoholic/drug addict   1 (2) 3 4 5
5. I have decided to quit drinking or doing drugs   (1) 2 3 4 5
6. I am currently attempting abstinence   1 (2) 3 4 5   **11**

7. I understand the characteristics about myself that get me in trouble   1 2 3 (4) 5
8. I know what my high risk behaviors are   1 2 3 (4) 5   **8**
9. I know what my strengths are that support recovery   1 2 (3) 4 5
10. I monitor my thoughts and feelings on a daily basis   1 (2) 3 4 5
11. I manage my self-defeating behaviors regularly   1 2 (3) 4 5
12. I take a personal inventory regularly and admit mistakes promptly   1 (2) 3 4 5   **10**

13. I am a totally different person now from when I was drinking/using   1 (2) 3 4 5
14. I have incorporated healthy and productive behaviors into my life   1 2 (3) 4 5
15. I go to self-help meetings such as AA   1 (2) 3 4 5   **7**

Client's name: _____ Date: _____

Paradigm: _____ Scale Category: _____

Georgi Distefano, LCSW & Melinda Hohman, Ph.D.

CASE 3
Paradigm Developmental Model of Treatment Scale
Georgi DiStefano, LCSW and Melinda Hohman, Ph.D.

Please answer each question as it applies to you right now, using the following scale:
1=Strongly Disagree   2= Disagree   3= Not sure   4=Agree   5=Strongly Agree

1. When I drink/use drugs, I frequently am unable to manage my use — 1 2 3 **(4)** 5
2. I now believe I have a problem with alcohol/drugs — 1 2 **(3)** 4 5
3. I realize I need help with my alcohol/drug problem — 1 **(2)** 3 4 5
4. I now believe that I am an alcoholic/drug addict — 1 **(2)** 3 4 5
5. I have decided to quit drinking or doing drugs — **(1)** 2 3 4 5
6. I am currently attempting abstinence — **(1)** 2 3 4 5   **13**

7. I understand the characteristics about myself that get me in trouble — 1 2 3 **(4)** 5
8. I know what my high risk behaviors are — 1 2 3 4 **(5)**   **9**
9. I know what my strengths are that support recovery — 1 2 **(3)** 4 5
10. I monitor my thoughts and feelings on a daily basis — 1 **(2)** 3 4 5
11. I manage my self-defeating behaviors regularly — 1 2 3 4 **(5)**
12. I take a personal inventory regularly and admit mistakes promptly — 1 2 3 4 **(5)**   **15**

13. I am a totally different person now from when I was drinking/using — 1 2 **(3)** 4 5
14. I have incorporated healthy and productive behaviors into my life — **(1)** 2 3 4 5
15. I go to self-help meetings such as AA — 1 2 3 **(4)** 5   **8**

Client's name: _____   Date: _____

Paradigm: _____   Scale Category: _____

Georgi Distefano, LCSW & Melinda Hohman, Ph.D.

CASE 4
Paradigm Developmental Model of Treatment Scale
Georgi DiStefano, LCSW and Melinda Hohman, Ph.D.

Please answer each question as it applies to you right now, using the following scale:
1=Strongly Disagree   2= Disagree   3= Not sure   4=Agree   5=Strongly Agree

1. When I drink/use drugs, I frequently am unable to manage my use   1 2 3 **(4)** 5
2. I now believe I have a problem with alcohol/drugs   1 2 3 **(4)** 5
3. I realize I need help with my alcohol/drug problem   1 2 3 **(4)** 5
4. I now believe that I am an alcoholic/drug addict   1 2 **(3)** 4 5
5. I have decided to quit drinking or doing drugs   1 2 **(3)** 4 5
6. I am currently attempting abstinence   1 2 3 **(4)** 5   **22**

7. I understand the characteristics about myself that get me in trouble   1 2 3 4 **(5)**
8. I know what my high risk behaviors are   1 2 3 4 **(5)**   **10**

9. I know what my strengths are that support recovery   1 2 3 **(4)** 5
10. I monitor my thoughts and feelings on a daily basis   1 2 3 **(4)** 5
11. I manage my self-defeating behaviors regularly   1 2 **(3)** 4 5
12. I take a personal inventory regularly and admit mistakes promptly   1 2 **(3)** 4 5   **14**

13. I am a totally different person now from when I was drinking/using   1 2 **(3)** 4 5
14. I have incorporated healthy and productive behaviors into my life   1 2 3 **(4)** 5
15. I go to self-help meetings such as AA   1 2 3 **(4)** 5   **11**

Client's name: _____ Date: _____

Paradigm: _____ Scale Category: _____

Georgi Distefano, LCSW & Melinda Hohman, Ph.D.

CASE 5
Paradigm Developmental Model of Treatment Scale
Georgi DiStefano, LCSW and Melinda Hohman, Ph.D.

Please answer each question as it applies to you right now, using the following scale:

1=Strongly Disagree   2= Disagree   3= Not sure   4=Agree   5=Strongly Agree

1. When I drink/use drugs, I frequently am unable to manage my use   1 2 3 4 **(5)**
2. I now believe I have a problem with alcohol/drugs   1 2 3 4 **(5)**
3. I realize I need help with my alcohol/drug problem   1 2 3 **(4)** 5
4. I now believe that I am an alcoholic/drug addict   1 2 3 4 **(5)**
5. I have decided to quit drinking or doing drugs   1 2 3 4 **(5)**
6. I am currently attempting abstinence   1 2 3 4 **(5)**   **29**

7. I understand the characteristics about myself that get me in trouble   1 2 3 **(4)** 5
8. I know what my high risk behaviors are   1 2 3 4 **(5)**   **9**

9. I know what my strengths are that support recovery   1 2 3 **(4)** 5
10. I monitor my thoughts and feelings on a daily basis   1 2 3 **(4)** 5
11. I manage my self-defeating behaviors regularly   1 2 3 **(4)** 5
12. I take a personal inventory regularly and admit mistakes promptly   1 2 3 **(4)** 5   **16**

13. I am a totally different person now from when I was drinking/using   1 2 3 **(4)** 5
14. I have incorporated healthy and productive behaviors into my life   1 2 3 **(4)** 5
15. I go to self-help meetings such as AA   1 2 3 **(4)** 5   **12**

Client's name: _____   Date: _____

Paradigm: _____   Scale Category: _____

Georgi Distefano, LCSW & Melinda Hohman, Ph.D.

CASE 6
Paradigm Developmental Model of Treatment Scale
Georgi DiStefano, LCSW and Melinda Hohman, Ph.D.

Please answer each question as it applies to you right now, using the following scale:
1=Strongly Disagree   2= Disagree   3= Not sure   4=Agree   5=Strongly Agree

1. When I drink/use drugs, I frequently am unable to manage my use — 1 2 3 ④ 5
2. I now believe I have a problem with alcohol/drugs — 1 2 3 ④ 5
3. I realize I need help with my alcohol/drug problem — 1 2 3 ④ 5
4. I now believe that I am an alcoholic/drug addict — 1 2 3 ④ 5
5. I have decided to quit drinking or doing drugs — 1 2 ③ 4 5
6. I am currently attempting abstinence — 1 2 3 ④ 5   **23**

7. I understand the characteristics about myself that get me in trouble — 1 2 3 ④ 5
8. I know what my high risk behaviors are — 1 2 ③ 4 5   **7**

9. I know what my strengths are that support recovery — 1 2 ③ 4 5
10. I monitor my thoughts and feelings on a daily basis — 1 2 3 ④ 5
11. I manage my self-defeating behaviors regularly — 1 2 ③ 4 5
12. I take a personal inventory regularly and admit mistakes promptly — 1 2 ③ 4 5   **13**

13. I am a totally different person now from when I was drinking/using — 1 2 ③ 4 5
14. I have incorporated healthy and productive behaviors into my life — 1 2 3 ④ 5
15. I go to self-help meetings such as AA — 1 2 3 ④ 5   **11**

Client's name: _____   Date: _____

Paradigm: _____   Scale Category: _____

Georgi Distefano, LCSW & Melinda Hohman, Ph.D.

CASE 7

Paradigm Developmental Model of Treatment Scale
Georgi DiStefano, LCSW and Melinda Hohman, Ph.D.

Please answer each question as it applies to you right now, using the following scale:

1=Strongly Disagree   2= Disagree   3= Not sure   4=Agree   5=Strongly Agree

#	Question	Response	Total
1.	When I drink/use drugs, I frequently am unable to manage my use	1 2 3 **(4)** 5	
2.	I now believe I have a problem with alcohol/drugs	1 2 3 **(4)** 5	
3.	I realize I need help with my alcohol/drug problem	1 2 **(3)** 4 5	
4.	I now believe that I am an alcoholic/drug addict	1 2 3 **(4)** 5	
5.	I have decided to quit drinking or doing drugs	1 **(2)** 3 4 5	
6.	I am currently attempting abstinence	1 **(2)** 3 4 5	**19**
7.	I understand the characteristics about myself that get me in trouble	1 2 3 **(4)** 5	
8.	I know what my high risk behaviors are	1 2 3 **(4)** 5	**8**
9.	I know what my strengths are that support recovery	1 2 **(3)** 4 5	
10.	I monitor my thoughts and feelings on a daily basis	1 2 3 **(4)** 5	
11.	I manage my self-defeating behaviors regularly	1 2 **(3)** 4 5	
12.	I take a personal inventory regularly and admit mistakes promptly	1 **(2)** 3 4 5	**12**
13.	I am a totally different person now from when I was drinking/using	1 **(2)** 3 4 5	
14.	I have incorporated healthy and productive behaviors into my life	1 2 3 **(4)** 5	
15.	I go to self-help meetings such as AA	1 2 3 **(4)** 5	**10**

Client's name: _____   Date: _____

Paradigm: _____   Scale Category: _____

Georgi Distefano, LCSW & Melinda Hohman, Ph.D.

CASE 8
Paradigm Developmental Model of Treatment Scale
Georgi DiStefano, LCSW and Melinda Hohman, Ph.D.

Please answer each question as it applies to you right now, using the following scale:
1=Strongly Disagree   2=Disagree   3=Not sure   4=Agree   5=Strongly Agree

1. When I drink/use drugs, I frequently am unable to manage my use — 1 2 3 4 **(5)**
2. I now believe I have a problem with alcohol/drugs — 1 2 3 4 **(5)**
3. I realize I need help with my alcohol/drug problem — 1 2 3 4 **(5)**
4. I now believe that I am an alcoholic/drug addict — 1 2 3 4 **(5)**
5. I have decided to quit drinking or doing drugs — 1 2 3 4 **(5)**
6. I am currently attempting abstinence — 1 2 3 **(4)** 5 **29**

7. I understand the characteristics about myself that get me in trouble — 1 2 3 4 **(5)**
8. I know what my high risk behaviors are — 1 2 3 4 **(5)** **10**
9. I know what my strengths are that support recovery — 1 2 3 **(4)** 5
10. I monitor my thoughts and feelings on a daily basis — 1 2 3 **(4)** 5
11. I manage my self-defeating behaviors regularly — 1 2 3 4 **(5)**
12. I take a personal inventory regularly and admit mistakes promptly — 1 2 3 **(4)** 5 **17**

13. I am a totally different person now from when I was drinking/using — 1 2 3 4 **(5)**
14. I have incorporated healthy and productive behaviors into my life — 1 2 3 4 **(5)**
15. I go to self-help meetings such as AA — 1 2 3 **(4)** 5 **14**

Client's name: _____   Date: _____

Paradigm: _____   Scale Category: _____

Georgi Distefano, LCSW & Melinda Hohman, Ph.D.

CASE 9

Paradigm Developmental Model of Treatment Scale
Georgi DiStefano, LCSW and Melinda Hohman, Ph.D.

Please answer each question as it applies to you right now, using the following scale:

| 1=Strongly Disagree | 2= Disagree | 3= Not sure | 4=Agree | 5=Strongly Agree |

1. When I drink/use drugs, I frequently am unable to manage my use — 1 2 3 4 **(5)**
2. I now believe I have a problem with alcohol/drugs — 1 2 3 4 **(5)**
3. I realize I need help with my alcohol/drug problem — 1 2 3 **(4)** 5
4. I now believe that I am an alcoholic/drug addict — 1 2 3 4 **(5)**
5. I have decided to quit drinking or doing drugs — 1 2 3 4 **(5)**
6. I am currently attempting abstinence — 1 2 3 4 **(5)**   **29**

7. I understand the characteristics about myself that get me in trouble — 1 2 3 **(4)** 5
8. I know what my high risk behaviors are — 1 2 3 4 **(5)**   **9**
9. I know what my strengths are that support recovery — 1 2 3 4 **(5)**
10. I monitor my thoughts and feelings on a daily basis — 1 2 **(3)** 4 5
11. I manage my self-defeating behaviors regularly — 1 2 **(3)** 4 5
12. I take a personal inventory regularly and admit mistakes promptly — 1 2 3 **(4)** 5   **15**

13. I am a totally different person now from when I was drinking/using — 1 2 3 4 **(5)**
14. I have incorporated healthy and productive behaviors into my life — 1 2 3 4 **(5)**
15. I go to self-help meetings such as AA — 1 2 3 4 **(5)**   **15**

Client's name: _____   Date: _____

Paradigm: _____   Scale Category: _____

Georgi Distefano, LCSW & Melinda Hohman, Ph.D.

CASE 10
Paradigm Developmental Model of Treatment Scale
Georgi DiStefano, LCSW and Melinda Hohman, Ph.D.

Please answer each question as it applies to you right now, using the following scale:
1=Strongly Disagree   2= Disagree   3= Not sure   4=Agree   5=Strongly Agree

#	Question	Response
1.	When I drink/use drugs, I frequently am unable to manage my use	1 2 3 4 (5)
2.	I now believe I have a problem with alcohol/drugs	1 2 3 4 (5)
3.	I realize I need help with my alcohol/drug problem	1 2 3 (4) 5
4.	I now believe that I am an alcoholic/drug addict	1 2 3 (4) 5
5.	I have decided to quit drinking or doing drugs	1 2 3 4 (5)
6.	I am currently attempting abstinence	1 2 3 4 (5) **28**
7.	I understand the characteristics about myself that get me in trouble	1 2 3 4 (5)
8.	I know what my high risk behaviors are	1 2 3 4 (5) **10**
9.	I know what my strengths are that support recovery	1 2 3 4 (5)
10.	I monitor my thoughts and feelings on a daily basis	1 2 3 4 (5)
11.	I manage my self-defeating behaviors regularly	1 2 3 4 (5)
12.	I take a personal inventory regularly and admit mistakes promptly	1 2 3 (4) 5 **19**
13.	I am a totally different person now from when I was drinking/using	1 2 3 (4) 5
14.	I have incorporated healthy and productive behaviors into my life	1 2 3 4 (5)
15.	I go to self-help meetings such as AA	1 2 3 4 (5) **14**

Client's name: _____   Date: _____

Paradigm: _____   Scale Category: _____

Georgi Distefano, LCSW & Melinda Hohman, Ph.D.

CASE 11

Paradigm Developmental Model of Treatment Scale
Georgi DiStefano, LCSW and Melinda Hohman, Ph.D.

Please answer each question as it applies to you right now, using the following scale:
1=Strongly Disagree   2=Disagree   3=Not sure   4=Agree   5=Strongly Agree

#	Question	Response
1.	When I drink/use drugs, I frequently am unable to manage my use	1 (2) 3 4 5
2.	I now believe I have a problem with alcohol/drugs	1 (2) 3 4 5
3.	I realize I need help with my alcohol/drug problem	1 (2) 3 4 5
4.	I now believe that I am an alcoholic/drug addict	(1) 2 3 4 5
5.	I have decided to quit drinking or doing drugs	1 (2) 3 4 5
6.	I am currently attempting abstinence	(1) 2 3 4 5 **10**
7.	I understand the characteristics about myself that get me in trouble	1 2 3 4 (5)
8.	I know what my high risk behaviors are	1 2 3 4 (5) **10**
9.	I know what my strengths are that support recovery	1 2 3 4 (5)
10.	I monitor my thoughts and feelings on a daily basis	1 2 3 4 (5)
11.	I manage my self-defeating behaviors regularly	1 2 3 (4) 5
12.	I take a personal inventory regularly and admit mistakes promptly	1 2 3 (4) 5 **18**
13.	I am a totally different person now from when I was drinking/using	(1) 2 3 4 5
14.	I have incorporated healthy and productive behaviors into my life	1 2 3 4 (5)
15.	I go to self-help meetings such as AA	1 2 3 4 (5) **11**

Client's name: _____   Date: _____

Paradigm: _____   Scale Category: _____

Georgi DiStefano, LCSW & Melinda Hohman, Ph.D.

CASE 12
Paradigm Developmental Model of Treatment Scale
Georgi DiStefano, LCSW and Melinda Hohman, Ph.D.

Please answer each question as it applies to you right now, using the following scale:
1=Strongly Disagree   2= Disagree   3= Not sure   4=Agree   5=Strongly Agree

1. When I drink/use drugs, I frequently am unable to manage my use	(1) 2 3 4 5	
2. I now believe I have a problem with alcohol/drugs	1 (2) 3 4 5	
3. I realize I need help with my alcohol/drug problem	1 (2) 3 4 5	
4. I now believe that I am an alcoholic/drug addict	(1) 2 3 4 5	
5. I have decided to quit drinking or doing drugs	1 (2) 3 4 5	
6. I am currently attempting abstinence	(1) 2 3 4 5	9
7. I understand the characteristics about myself that get me in trouble	1 2 3 4 (5)	
8. I know what my high risk behaviors are	1 2 3 4 (5)	10
9. I know what my strengths are that support recovery	1 2 3 (4) 5	
10. I monitor my thoughts and feelings on a daily basis	1 2 3 4 (5)	
11. I manage my self-defeating behaviors regularly	1 2 (3) 4 5	
12. I take a personal inventory regularly and admit mistakes promptly	1 2 3 (4) 5	16
13. I am a totally different person now from when I was drinking/using	1 2 (3) 4 5	
14. I have incorporated healthy and productive behaviors into my life	1 2 (3) 4 5	
15. I go to self-help meetings such as AA	1 2 3 4 (5)	11

Client's name: _____   Date: _____

Paradigm: _____   Scale Category: _____

Georgi Distefano, LCSW & Melinda Hohman, Ph.D.

CASE 13
Paradigm Developmental Model of Treatment Scale
Georgi DiStefano, LCSW and Melinda Hohman, Ph.D.

Please answer each question as it applies to you right now, using the following scale:
1=Strongly Disagree   2= Disagree   3= Not sure   4=Agree   5=Strongly Agree

1. When I drink/use drugs, I frequently am unable to manage my use   1 2 ③ 4 5
2. I now believe I have a problem with alcohol/drugs   1 2 ③ 4 5
3. I realize I need help with my alcohol/drug problem   1 2 ③ 4 5
4. I now believe that I am an alcoholic/drug addict   1 ② 3 4 5
5. I have decided to quit drinking or doing drugs   ① 2 3 4 5
6. I am currently attempting abstinence   ① 2 3 4 5   **13**

7. I understand the characteristics about myself that get me in trouble   1 2 3 4 ⑤
8. I know what my high risk behaviors are   1 2 3 4 ⑤   **10**

9. I know what my strengths are that support recovery   1 2 ③ 4 5
10. I monitor my thoughts and feelings on a daily basis   1 2 ③ 4 5
11. I manage my self-defeating behaviors regularly   1 2 ③ 4 5
12. I take a personal inventory regularly and admit mistakes promptly   1 2 3 ④ 5   **13**

13. I am a totally different person now from when I was drinking/using   1 2 ③ 4 5
14. I have incorporated healthy and productive behaviors into my life   1 2 3 ④ 5
15. I go to self-help meetings such as AA   1 2 3 ④ 5   **11**

Client's name: _____   Date: _____

Paradigm: _____   Scale Category: _____

Georgi Distefano, LCSW & Melinda Hohman, Ph.D.

CASE 14
Paradigm Developmental Model of Treatment Scale
Georgi DiStefano, LCSW and Melinda Hohman, Ph.D.

Please answer each question as it applies to you right now, using the following scale:
1=Strongly Disagree 2=Disagree 3=Not sure 4=Agree 5=Strongly Agree

1. When I drink/use drugs, I frequently am unable to manage my use — 1 2 ③ 4 5
2. I now believe I have a problem with alcohol/drugs — 1 2 ③ 4 5
3. I realize I need help with my alcohol/drug problem — 1 ② 3 4 5
4. I now believe that I am an alcoholic/drug addict — 1 ② 3 4 5
5. I have decided to quit drinking or doing drugs — 1 ② 3 4 5
6. I am currently attempting abstinence — 1 ② 3 4 5 **14**

7. I understand the characteristics about myself that get me in trouble — 1 2 3 4 ⑤
8. I know what my high risk behaviors are — 1 2 3 4 ⑤ **10**

9. I know what my strengths are that support recovery — 1 2 ③ 4 5
10. I monitor my thoughts and feelings on a daily basis — 1 2 3 ④ 5
11. I manage my self-defeating behaviors regularly — 1 2 3 ④ 5
12. I take a personal inventory regularly and admit mistakes promptly — 1 2 3 ④ 5 **15**

13. I am a totally different person now from when I was drinking/using — 1 ② 3 4 5
14. I have incorporated healthy and productive behaviors into my life — 1 2 3 ④ 5
15. I go to self-help meetings such as AA — 1 2 3 ④ 5 **10**

Client's name: _____ Date: _____

Paradigm: _____ Scale Category: _____

Georgi Distefano, LCSW & Melinda Hohman, Ph.D.

CASE 15

Paradigm Developmental Model of Treatment Scale
Georgi DiStefano, LCSW and Melinda Hohman, Ph.D.

Please answer each question as it applies to you right now, using the following scale:
1=Strongly Disagree   2=Disagree   3=Not sure   4=Agree   5=Strongly Agree

#	Question	Response
1.	When I drink/use drugs, I frequently am unable to manage my use	1 2 3 **(4)** 5
2.	I now believe I have a problem with alcohol/drugs	1 2 3 **(4)** 5
3.	I realize I need help with my alcohol/drug problem	1 **(2)** 3 4 5
4.	I now believe that I am an alcoholic/drug addict	1 2 3 **(4)** 5
5.	I have decided to quit drinking or doing drugs	1 2 3 4 **(5)**
6.	I am currently attempting abstinence	1 2 3 4 **(5)** **24**
7.	I understand the characteristics about myself that get me in trouble	1 2 3 4 **(5)**
8.	I know what my high risk behaviors are	1 2 3 4 **(5)** **10**
9.	I know what my strengths are that support recovery	1 2 3 4 **(5)**
10.	I monitor my thoughts and feelings on a daily basis	1 2 **(3)** 4 5
11.	I manage my self-defeating behaviors regularly	1 2 3 4 **(5)**
12.	I take a personal inventory regularly and admit mistakes promptly	1 2 3 **(4)** 5 **17**
13.	I am a totally different person now from when I was drinking/using	1 **(2)** 3 4 5
14.	I have incorporated healthy and productive behaviors into my life	1 2 3 4 **(5)**
15.	I go to self-help meetings such as AA	1 2 3 **(4)** 5 **11**

Client's name: _____   Date: _____

Paradigm: _____   Scale Category: _____

Georgi Distefano, LCSW & Melinda Hohman, Ph.D.

CASE 16
Paradigm Developmental Model of Treatment Scale
Georgi DiStefano, LCSW and Melinda Hohman, Ph.D.

Please answer each question as it applies to you right now, using the following scale:
1=Strongly Disagree   2= Disagree   3= Not sure   4=Agree   5=Strongly Agree

1. When I drink/use drugs, I frequently am unable to manage my use	1 2 3 4 ⑤
2. I now believe I have a problem with alcohol/drugs	1 2 3 ④ 5
3. I realize I need help with my alcohol/drug problem	1 2 3 ④ 5
4. I now believe that I am an alcoholic/drug addict	1 2 3 4 ⑤
5. I have decided to quit drinking or doing drugs	1 ② 3 4 5
6. I am currently attempting abstinence	1 2 ③ 4 5 **23**
7. I understand the characteristics about myself that get me in trouble	1 2 3 ④ 5
8. I know what my high risk behaviors are	1 2 3 ④ 5 **8**
9. I know what my strengths are that support recovery	1 ② 3 4 5
10. I monitor my thoughts and feelings on a daily basis	1 2 3 4 ⑤
11. I manage my self-defeating behaviors regularly	1 ② 3 4 5
12. I take a personal inventory regularly and admit mistakes promptly	1 ② 3 4 5 **11**
13. I am a totally different person now from when I was drinking/using	1 2 3 ④ 5
14. I have incorporated healthy and productive behaviors into my life	1 2 ③ 4 5
15. I go to self-help meetings such as AA	1 2 ③ 4 5 **10**

Client's name: _____   Date: _____

Paradigm: _____   Scale Category: _____

Georgi Distefano, LCSW & Melinda Hohman, Ph.D.

CASE 17
Paradigm Developmental Model of Treatment Scale
Georgi DiStefano, LCSW and Melinda Hohman, Ph.D.

Please answer each question as it applies to you right now, using the following scale:
1=Strongly Disagree   2= Disagree   3= Not sure   4=Agree   5=Strongly Agree

1. When I drink/use drugs, I frequently am unable to manage my use — 1 2 3 4 **(5)**
2. I now believe I have a problem with alcohol/drugs — 1 2 **(3)** 4 5
3. I realize I need help with my alcohol/drug problem — 1 2 3 4 **(5)**
4. I now believe that I am an alcoholic/drug addict — 1 2 3 4 **(5)**
5. I have decided to quit drinking or doing drugs — 1 2 3 4 **(5)**
6. I am currently attempting abstinence — 1 2 3 4 **(5)**   **28**

7. I understand the characteristics about myself that get me in trouble — 1 2 3 4 **(5)**
8. I know what my high risk behaviors are — 1 2 3 4 **(5)**   **10**

9. I know what my strengths are that support recovery — 1 2 3 4 **(5)**
10. I monitor my thoughts and feelings on a daily basis — 1 2 3 **(4)** 5
11. I manage my self-defeating behaviors regularly — 1 2 3 **(4)** 5
12. I take a personal inventory regularly and admit mistakes promptly — 1 2 3 **(4)** 5   **17**

13. I am a totally different person now from when I was drinking/using — 1 2 3 4 **(5)**
14. I have incorporated healthy and productive behaviors into my life — 1 2 3 4 **(5)**
15. I go to self-help meetings such as AA — 1 2 3 4 **(5)**   **15**

Client's name: _____   Date: _____

Paradigm: _____   Scale Category: _____

CASE 18
Paradigm Developmental Model of Treatment Scale
Georgi DiStefano, LCSW and Melinda Hohman, Ph.D.

Please answer each question as it applies to you right now, using the following scale:
1=Strongly Disagree   2= Disagree   3= Not sure   4=Agree   5=Strongly Agree

#	Question	Response
1.	When I drink/use drugs, I frequently am unable to manage my use	1 2 3 4 **(5)**
2.	I now believe I have a problem with alcohol/drugs	1 2 3 4 **(5)**
3.	I realize I need help with my alcohol/drug problem	1 2 3 **(4)** 5
4.	I now believe that I am an alcoholic/drug addict	1 2 3 **(4)** 5
5.	I have decided to quit drinking or doing drugs	1 2 3 4 **(5)**
6.	I am currently attempting abstinence	1 2 3 4 **(5)** **28**
7.	I understand the characteristics about myself that get me in trouble	1 2 3 4 **(5)**
8.	I know what my high risk behaviors are	1 2 3 4 **(5)** **10**
9.	I know what my strengths are that support recovery	1 2 3 **(4)** 5
10.	I monitor my thoughts and feelings on a daily basis	1 2 3 **(4)** 5
11.	I manage my self-defeating behaviors regularly	1 2 3 **(4)** 5
12.	I take a personal inventory regularly and admit mistakes promptly	1 2 3 **(4)** 5 **16**
13.	I am a totally different person now from when I was drinking/using	1 2 3 **(4)** 5
14.	I have incorporated healthy and productive behaviors into my life	1 2 3 4 **(5)**
15.	I go to self-help meetings such as AA	1 2 3 4 **(5)** **14**

Client's name: _____   Date: _____

Paradigm: _____   Scale Category: _____

Georgi Distefano, LCSW & Melinda Hohman, Ph.D.

CASE 19

Paradigm Developmental Model of Treatment Scale
Georgi DiStefano, LCSW and Melinda Hohman, Ph.D.

Please answer each question as it applies to you right now, using the following scale:
1=Strongly Disagree   2= Disagree   3= Not sure   4=Agree   5=Strongly Agree

1. When I drink/use drugs, I frequently am unable to manage my use   1 2 3 **(4)** 5
2. I now believe I have a problem with alcohol/drugs   1 2 3 **(4)** 5
3. I realize I need help with my alcohol/drug problem   1 2 3 **(4)** 5
4. I now believe that I am an alcoholic/drug addict   1 2 3 **(4)** 5
5. I have decided to quit drinking or doing drugs   1 2 3 **(4)** 5
6. I am currently attempting abstinence   1 2 3 **(4)** 5   **24**

7. I understand the characteristics about myself that get me in trouble   1 2 3 4 **(5)**
8. I know what my high risk behaviors are   1 2 3 **(4)** 5   **9**

9. I know what my strengths are that support recovery   1 2 **(3)** 4 5
10. I monitor my thoughts and feelings on a daily basis   1 2 3 **(4)** 5
11. I manage my self-defeating behaviors regularly   1 2 **(3)** 4 5
12. I take a personal inventory regularly and admit mistakes promptly   1 2 **(3)** 4 5   **13**

13. I am a totally different person now from when I was drinking/using   1 2 **(3)** 4 5
14. I have incorporated healthy and productive behaviors into my life   1 2 3 **(4)** 5
15. I go to self-help meetings such as AA   1 2 3 **(4)** 5   **11**

Client's name: _____   Date: _____

Paradigm: _____   Scale Category: _____

Georgi Distefano, LCSW & Melinda Hohman, Ph.D.

CASE 20
Paradigm Developmental Model of Treatment Scale
Georgi DiStefano, LCSW and Melinda Hohman, Ph.D.

Please answer each question as it applies to you right now, using the following scale:
1=Strongly Disagree   2= Disagree   3= Not sure   4=Agree   5=Strongly Agree

1. When I drink/use drugs, I frequently am unable to manage my use — 1 2 3 **(4)** 5
2. I now believe I have a problem with alcohol/drugs — 1 2 3 4 **(5)**
3. I realize I need help with my alcohol/drug problem — 1 2 3 **(4)** 5
4. I now believe that I am an alcoholic/drug addict — 1 2 3 4 **(5)**
5. I have decided to quit drinking or doing drugs — 1 2 3 4 **(5)**
6. I am currently attempting abstinence — 1 2 3 **(4)** 5   **27**

7. I understand the characteristics about myself that get me in trouble — 1 2 3 **(4)** 5
8. I know what my high risk behaviors are — 1 2 3 **(4)** 5   **8**
9. I know what my strengths are that support recovery — 1 2 3 **(4)** 5
10. I monitor my thoughts and feelings on a daily basis — 1 2 3 **(4)** 5
11. I manage my self-defeating behaviors regularly — 1 2 3 **(4)** 5
12. I take a personal inventory regularly and admit mistakes promptly — 1 2 3 **(4)** 5   **16**

13. I am a totally different person now from when I was drinking/using — 1 2 3 **(4)** 5
14. I have incorporated healthy and productive behaviors into my life — 1 2 3 **(4)** 5
15. I go to self-help meetings such as AA — 1 2 3 **(4)** 5   **12**

Client's name: _____   Date: _____

Paradigm: _____   Scale Category: _____

Georgi Distefano, LCSW & Melinda Hohman, Ph.D.

PRACTICE SCALES RESULTS – SCORING GRID

		Paradigm		Scale Category
Case	1	Taking Responsibility	II	Accepting/Implementing
Case	2	Problem Recognition	I	Disinterested
Case	3	Problem Recognition	I	Contemplating
Case	4	Problem Recognition	I	Contemplating
Case	5	Self-Regulation	III	Consistent Action
Case	6	Problem Recognition	I	Contemplating
Case	7	Problem Recognition	I	Contemplating
Case	8	Transformation	IV	Transformation or Overconfident *
Case	9	Taking Responsibility	II	Accepting/Implementing
Case	10	Transformation	IV	Transformation or Overconfident *
Case	11	Problem Recognition	I	Disinterested
Case	12	Problem Recognition	I	Disinterested
Case	13	Problem Recognition	I	Contemplating
Case	14	Problem Recognition	I	Contemplating
Case	15	Taking Responsibility	II	Accepting/Implementing
Case	16	Problem Recognition	I	Contemplating
Case	17	Transformation	IV	Transformation or Overconfident *
Case	18	Self-Regulation	III	Consistent Action
Case	19	Taking Responsibility	II	Accepting/Implementing
Case	20	Self-Regulation	III	Consistent Action

* Must have further assessment

Georgi Distefano, LCSW & Melinda Hohman, Ph.D.

CLINICAL GOALS AND INTERVENTIONS FOR PARADIGM I

Paradigm Developmental Model

Client Name: _____ Cl #: _____ Counselor: _____

Paradigm Stage	Client's Issues/Motivators	Date	Counselor Interventions
Paradigm 1: Problem Recognition and Acceptance of Help ***Clinical Goals:*** • Determine client motivators • Realistic evaluation of AOD issues • Identification high-risk behaviors • Identification of co-occurring problems/disorders • High-risk prevention planning • Harm reduction plan/ Initiation of abstinence • Willingness to accept formal AOD treatment ***Interventions:*** 1. Providing Assessment Feedback 2. Motivators and Goals 3. Loss/Grief/Anger/Resentment 4. Family/Friends: Attitude/Support Assessment: Identification of High-Risk Behaviors **Selecting Interventions** 5. General MI Discussion 6. Looking Forward/Looking Back/Consequence History 7. Decisional Balance 8. Personal Values Card Sort 9. Personal Ruler 10. Mutual Support Group and AA 11. Identifying Cravings/Urges and Triggers: Playgrounds, Playmates and Playthings 12. Determining Unmanageability			

Georgi Distefano, LCSW & Melinda Hohman, Ph.D.

PARADIGM I EXERCISES

PARADIGM I
Exercise

Client Name: _____

MOTIVATORS AND GOALS

1) Your reaction to the assessment:

___ a) I agree
___ b) I do not agree
___ c) I'm undecided, need further consideration

2) My goal regarding my drinking/drug use is:

1) Controlled use: _____

2) Abstinence: _____

3) Recovery: _____

4) Other: _____

3) My top three motivators for being successful with my goal are:

1) _____
Reason? _____

2) _____
Reason? _____

3) _____
Reason? _____

Georgi Distefano, LCSW & Melinda Hohman, Ph.D.

PARADIGM I
Exercise

Client Name: _____

My experiences with these issues are:

Loss/Grief _____
_____
_____

Anger _____
_____
_____

Resentment Issues _____
_____
_____

Family _____
_____
_____

Friends _____
_____
_____

Support Systems _____
_____
_____

Georgi Distefano, LCSW & Melinda Hohman, Ph.D.

PARADIGM I
Exercise

Client Name: _____

IDENTIFICATION OF HIGH-RISK BEHAVIORS

1) My goal for my drinking/drug use is:

a) Controlled use: _____

b) Abstinence: _____

c) Recovery: _____

d) Other: _____

2) My motivators for being successful with my goal are:

1) _____

2) _____

3) _____

3) These situations or behaviors are high-risk for me:

1) _____
Reason? _____
_____

2) _____
Reason? _____
_____

3) _____
Reason? _____
_____

Georgi Distefano, LCSW & Melinda Hohman, Ph.D.

ANY PARADIGM
Exercise 1

MI DISCUSSION USING CHANGE-TALK QUESTIONS

What would it take for you to seriously think about _____?

What are your specific thoughts about "change"?

Would it be alright if we talked about_____?

If you were to consider change, how would you do it? What ideas do you have? When would be a good time to start?

How would you know that _____things aren't working? That alcohol/substances are an issue? That change makes sense? It's time?

Let's *pretend* or let's *fantasize* for a moment that you made the changes you're talking about: _____What would this look like to you? How could you get closer to that?

If X months went by and this didn't change, what would that be like?

If you decided to make a change in X, regardless of the "how to" to accomplish it, what would that be like?

When you look ahead to the end of our work together (X months from now), how would you like your life to be different?

If our work together goes exactly the way you would hope, what would things be like once we're finished?

What would have to happen for your life to change that way?

What is standing in the way of changing your life so it's the way you want it to be?

Are you really sure you want to do this?

What are the good things about what you're doing now? What do you really like about it? What would be the advantages of continuing the same behavior? What might make you think that changing would be the last thing you might want to do?

If we had a magic wand and could make things different, what would you do differently? How would you feel different?

What is currently impossible to do, that if it were possible, might change everything?

If you were in my shoes, what helpful question would you ask yourself about _____?

If you were to make a change, what's your theory on the best way to do it for who you are?

What inner strengths and resources do you have that would most support you in making and sustaining change?

Miller, W.R. & Rollnick S.

Georgi Distefano, LCSW & Melinda Hohman, Ph.D.

ANY PARADIGM
Exercise 2

ADDITIONAL CHANGE-TALK QUESTIONS

In the change we are talking about, what would be the next logical step to take?

What would be the advantages of taking this step?

What would be the disadvantages of taking this step?

Would you like to take this step and implement your plan?

Are you willing to make a commitment to take this step?

Ask the client to summarize the agreement.

Georgi Distefano, LCSW & Melinda Hohman, Ph.D.

PARADIGM I
Exercise

CONSEQUENCE HISTORY
MY DRINKING / DRUG USE

Client Name: _____

Onset Age:	Age:	Age:
Motivation:	Motivation:	Motivation:
Use pattern:	Use pattern:	Use pattern:
Environmental Influences:	Environmental Influences:	Environmental Influences:
Consequences/Problems caused by AOD:	Consequences/Problems caused by AOD:	Consequences/Problems cause by AOD:

USE PATTERN = alcohol or other drugs, quantities, frequencies and progression

Georgi Distefano, LCSW & Melinda Hohman, Ph.D.

PARADIGM I

Exercise

LOOKING FORWARD

Client Name: _____

Where am I today?	Where will I be in five years with no changes?	Where will I be in five years with changes?
Age	Age	Age
Use pattern	Anticipate use pattern (Remember progressive process)	Problems resolved because of changes
Consequences/Problems caused by AOD	Consequences/Problems caused by AOD	Consequences/Problems caused by AOD
Describe quality of life	Describe quality of life	Describe quality of life

Adapted from: Miller, W.R., ed. COMBINE Monograph Series, Volume 1. Combined Behavioral Intervention Manual: A Clinical Research Guide for Therapists Treating People with Alcohol Abuse and Dependence. DHHS Publication N0. (NIH) 04-5288. Bethesda, MD: NIAAA, 2004.

Georgi Distefano, LCSW & Melinda Hohman, Ph.D.

PARADIGM I
Exercise

Client Name: _____

DECISIONAL BALANCE WORKSHEET
Combined Behavioral Intervention Manual

The change is: _____

Cons (Reasons Not to Change)	Pros (Reasons to Change)
1 Good things about continuing to drink as before	**2 Not-so-good things about drinking**
3 Not-so-good things about changing my drinking	**4 Good things about changing my drinking**

Adapted from: Miller, W.R., ed. COMBINE Monograph Series, Volume 1. Combined Behavioral Intervention Manual: A Clinical Research Guide for Therapists Treating People with Alcohol Abuse and Dependence. DHHS Publication N0. (NIH) 04-5288. Bethesda, MD: NIAAA, 2004.

Georgi Distefano, LCSW & Melinda Hohman, Ph.D.

PARADIGM I
Exercise

Client Name: _____

CARD SORT ITEMS

Which areas are related to your drinking and/or drug use (both positive and negative)?

LIFE AREAS	YES	RANK
Friends and social life		
Job/work		
Living situation		
Money, financial security		
Education and learning		
Leisure time and fun		
Mood and self-esteem		
Anger and arguments		
Stress and anxiety		
Physical health		
Spirituality		
Love and affection		
Family relationships		
Relationship with spouse/partner		
Sexuality		
Eating, weight		
Physical activity, exercise		
Giving/caring for others		
Mental ability, memory		
Personal safety, security		

CHECK YES ANSWERS TO QUESTIONS

RANK CLIENT'S TOP FIVE SELECTIONS

Adapted from: Miller, W.R., ed. COMBINE Monograph Series, Volume 1. Combined Behavioral Intervention Manual: A Clinical Research Guide for Therapists Treating People with Alcohol Abuse and Dependence. DHHS Publication N0. (NIH) 04-5288. Bethesda, MD: NIAAA, 2004.

Georgi Distefano, LCSW & Melinda Hohman, Ph.D.

PARADIGM I

Exercise

Client Name: _____

PERSONAL RULER WORKSHEET
Combined Behavioral Intervention Manual

Behavior: _____

Importance Ruler

0	1	2	3	4	5	6	7	8	9	10
Not at all important		Somewhat important		Fairly important		Important		Very important		Extremely important

Confidence Ruler

0	1	2	3	4	5	6	7	8	9	10
Not at all confident		Somewhat confident		Fairly confident		Confident		Very confident		Certain

Readiness Ruler

0	1	2	3	4	5	6	7	8	9	10
Not at all ready		Somewhat ready		Fairly ready		Ready		Very ready		Completely ready

Miller, W.R., ed. COMBINE Monograph Series, Volume 1. Combined Behavioral Intervention Manual: A Clinical Research Guide for Therapists Treating People with Alcohol Abuse and Dependence. DHHS Publication N0. (NIH) 04-5288. Bethesda, MD: NIAAA, 2004.

Georgi Distefano, LCSW & Melinda Hohman, Ph.D.

PARADIGM I
Exercise

Client Name: _____

REACTIONS TO AA OR OTHER SELF-HELP MEETINGS

Name of meeting: _____

Location: _____

Type of meeting (open discussion, speaker, etc): _____

1. Things I feel were negative, useless, or irrelevant:

   a) _____
   _____

   b) _____
   _____

   c) _____
   _____

2. Things that were useful, productive or encouraging about the meeting(s) I attended:

   a) _____
   _____

   b) _____
   _____

   c) _____
   _____

Georgi Distefano, LCSW & Melinda Hohman, Ph.D.

PARADIGM I
Exercise

IDENTIFYING CRAVINGS/URGES AND TRIGGERS

Client Name: _____

Circle those triggers that are relevant to you:

External Triggers (Playgrounds, Playmates and Playthings)	Internal Triggers (Emotions Sensations)	
Exposure to alcohol/drugs/high risk behavior	Anxiety	When/Why: _____
When/Where: _____	Elation	When/Why: _____
Seeing other people drinking/using	Fatigue/sleep loss	When/Why: _____
When/Where: _____	Happiness	When/Why: _____
People/things associated with drinking/drug use	Stress	When/Why: _____
Who/When/Where: _____	Shakes/tremors	When/Why: _____
Particular days or times when drinking/drug use occurred	Excitement	When/Why: _____
What/When: _____	Frustration	When/Why: _____
Events/situations	Anger	When/Why: _____
When/Where: _____	Loneliness/boredom	*When/Why:* _____
Music/playgrounds	Grief/sadness	*When/Why:* _____
When/Where: _____	Depression	*When/Why:* _____
Sexual dynamics - visual stimuli	Self-doubt/guilt	*When/Why:* _____
When/Where: _____	Other: _____	*When/Why:* _____
Other		
When/Where: _____		

Georgi Distefano, LCSW & Melinda Hohman, Ph.D.

Adapted from: Miller, W.R.., ed. COMBINE Monograph Series, Volume 1. Combined Behavioral Intervention Manual: A Clinical Research Guide for Therapists Treating People with Alcohol Abuse and Dependence. DHHS Publication N0. (NIH) 04-5288. Bethesda, MD: NIAAA, 2004.

PARADIGM I
Exercise

Client Name: _____

DETERMINING UNMANAGEABILITY

Identify times when your substance use has become out of control and resulted in negative consequences. _____
_____
_____
_____
_____
_____
_____
_____
_____
_____

Looking back at these incidents, do you think you were <u>powerless</u> in regards to controlling your use?

If yes, why. _____
_____
_____
_____
_____
_____
_____
_____

If no, why. _____
_____
_____
_____
_____
_____
_____
_____

Georgi Distefano, LCSW & Melinda Hohman, Ph.D.

Did you make any promises to yourself or others after these incidents? What were they?

Did you keep these promises to yourself or others? Yes/No. Explain

In what other areas do you feel your life has become off track or unmanageable?

In reflecting on the above questions – Do you feel you need or want to make any commitments to change at this time? What are they?

PARADIGM II EXERCISES

Clinical Goals and Interventions for Paradigm II
Paradigm Developmental Model

Client Name:_____ Cl #:_____ Counselor:_____

Paradigm Stage	Client's Issues/Motivators	Date	Counselor Interventions
Paradigm 2: Acceptance of Responsibility ***Clinical Goals:*** • Revisit goals and motivators • Identification of self-sabotaging behaviors • Identification of strengths/resiliencies • Managing co-occurring disorders • Relapse prevention plans • Practice alternative behaviors ***Interventions:*** 1. Developing Change Plan 2. What Gets In The Way? 3. Supporting Goals/Motivators 4. My Cultural Influences 5. Trigger Response Plan 6. Coping With Cravings/Urges 7. Social Pressure Situations. Exercise 1 & 2. 8. Learning From Collective Wisdom 9. Self-Examination and Communication Styles 10. Old/New Behaviors 11. What Is In My Control? 12. Both Sides Of The Street			

Georgi Distefano, LCSW & Melinda Hohman, Ph.D.

PARADIGM II
Exercise

Client Name: _____

SELF-EXAMINATION

STRENGTHS	**LIABILITIES**
These behaviors and attitudes support my goal and motivators: 1. _____ 2. _____ 3. _____	These behaviors and attitudes can work against me: 1. _____ 2. _____ 3. _____
ACTIONS TO SUPPORT MY STRENGTHS 1. _____ 2. _____ 3. _____	**ACTIONS TO CHANGE MY LIABILITIES** 1. _____ 2. _____ 3. _____

Georgi Distefano, LCSW & Melinda Hohman, Ph.D.

PARADIGM II
Exercise

Client Name: _____

WHAT IS MY COMMUNICATION STYLE?

COMMUNICATOR STYLE			
	AGGRESSIVE	Get the job done	Take care of one's own needs, even at the expense of others
		Make others listen	Disregard rights of others
		Seek to be powerful and in control of situation	Shame / bully
	PASSIVE	Avoid conflict	Give up rights
		Go along	Keep silent
		Keep things smooth	Bottle up feelings
	ASSERTIVE	Take responsibility	Respect rights of others
		Express oneself directly	Listen to others
		Are clear about feelings	Remain flexible

1. I think my style is _____

2. The benefits of this style for me are:
   a. _____
   b. _____
   c. _____

3. The limits of this style for me are:
   a. _____
   b. _____
   c. _____

4. I want to become more _____

5. Some ways I can do this are:
   a. _____
   b. _____
   c. _____

Georgi Distefano, LCSW & Melinda Hohman, Ph.D.

PARADIGM II
Exercise

Client Name: _____

HIGH-RISK BEHAVIOR CHANGE PLAN WORKSHEET

1. The change I want to make is:
   _____
   _____
   _____

2. The most important reasons I want to make this change are:
   _____
   _____
   _____
   _____

3. The steps I plan to take in changing are:
   _____
   _____
   _____
   _____
   _____
   _____

4. The ways other people can help me are:
   _____
   _____
   _____
   _____
   _____

5. I will know my plan is working if:
   _____
   _____
   _____
   _____
   _____

6. Some things that could interfere with my plan are:
   _____
   _____
   _____
   _____
   _____
   _____

Georgi Distefano, LCSW & Melinda Hohman, Ph.D.

PARADIGM II
Exercise

Client Name: _____

WHAT GETS IN THE WAY?

Sometimes when people have quit drinking or using drugs and are working a recovery program, they still feel like things are still "just not right." These things can be:

NEGATIVE THOUGHTS **POSITIVE THOUGHTS** **OTHERS' BEHAVIORS**

MY OWN BEHAVIORS **NEGATIVE FEELINGS POSITIVE** **FEELINGS**

RELATIONSHIPS FRIEN **DS** **PLAYGROUNDS/HANGOUTS**

WORK/SCHOOL GRIEF **RIGID THINKING**

Think through some of these things and list them with your counselor.

What Might Be Getting in the Way?   Rating

1. _____ _____

2. _____ _____

3. _____ _____

4. _____ _____

5. _____ _____

6. _____ _____

7. _____ _____

8. _____ _____

9. _____ _____

10. _____ _____

After you are done, please rate the importance of each item in terms of your need to address it with your counselor:

    4   Extremely important
    3   Important
    2   Somewhat important
    1   Not that important

Georgi Distefano, LCSW & Melinda Hohman, Ph.D.

PARADIGM II
Exercise

Client Name: _____

REVISITING MY GOAL AND MOTIVATORS

My goal regarding my drinking/drug use is:
1) Abstinence
2) Recovery
3) Other

My top three motivators for success with my AOD issues are:

1 _____
2 _____
3 _____

Behaviors that support my goal(s) and motivators are:

1 _____
Why? _____
2 _____
Why? _____
3 _____
Why? _____

Behaviors that could sabotage my goal(s) and motivators are:

1 _____
Why? _____
2 _____
Why? _____
3 _____
Why? _____

Georgi Distefano, LCSW & Melinda Hohman, Ph.D.

PARADIGM II
Exercise 1

Client Name: _____

MY CULTURAL INFLUENCES
How has my culture influenced me?

Select the issues regarding your culture that most resonate with you in either a positive or negative way.

Issues: Gender – Rituals – Holidays/Traditions – Foods/Festivals – Community Values – Art/Music – Religion/Spirituality – Family Values – Attitudes Towards Mental Health – Attitudes Toward Alcohol/Drugs Use – Other Issues

Positive	Negative
Issue:	**Issue:**
Why?:	Why?:
Issue:	**Issue:**
Why?:	Why?:
Issue:	**Issue:**
Why?:	Why?:

Georgi Distefano, LCSW & Melinda Hohman, Ph.D.

PARADIGM II
Exercise 2

Client Name: _____

MY CULTURAL INFLUENCES
Reducing the Negative Impact

Now that you have determined the cultural issue(s) that have a negative impact on you, develop a plan on how to eliminate or reduce their negative impact.

Issue: _____
Issue: _____
Issue: _____

Things I can do to eliminate or reduce the negative impact of this issue.

1. _____
_____
_____
_____

2. _____
_____
_____
_____

3. _____
_____
_____
_____

Georgi Distefano, LCSW & Melinda Hohman, Ph.D.

PARADIGM II
Exercise 3

Client Name: _____

MY CULTURAL INFLUENCES
Positive Impact

Select cultural issues that you feel support your growth and development.

How would you like to become more involved with these areas?

Issue: _____
Issue: _____
Issue: _____

Plans to increase activity in these areas:

1.
   _____
   _____
   _____

2.
   _____
   _____
   _____

3.
   _____
   _____
   _____

Georgi Distefano, LCSW & Melinda Hohman, Ph.D.

PARADIGM II

Client Name: _____

URGE MONITORING CARD

Date/Time	Situation	Urge to Use 0-100	Length of urge*	How I Responded	Strategy

Four basic strategies for coping with external triggers:

1. Avoid
2. Escape
3. Distract
4. Endure

*How long was the urge at its most intense?

Adapted from Miller, W.R., ed. COMBINE Monograph Series, Volume 1. Combined Behavioral Intervention Manual: A Clinical Research Guide for Therapists Treating People with Alcohol Abuse and Dependence. DHHS Publication N0. (NIH) 04-5288. Bethesda, MD: NIAAA, 2004.

Georgi Distefano, LCSW & Melinda Hohman, Ph.D.

Client Name: _____

PARADIGM II
Exercise 2

COPING WITH TRIGGERS
"TRIGGER RESPONSE PLAN"

My trigger is: _____

When this trigger is anticipated or activated, the actions I will take are:

a) _____
b) _____
c) _____

My trigger is: _____

When this trigger is anticipated or activated, the actions I will take are:

a) _____
b) _____
c) _____

My trigger is: _____

When this trigger is anticipated or activated, the actions I will take are:

a) _____
b) _____
c) _____

Georgi Distefano, LCSW & Melinda Hohman, Ph.D.

PARADIGM II
Exercise 1

CHECKLIST OF SOCIAL PRESSURE SITUATIONS

Client Name: _____

To what extent do you expect that these situations could pose a problem for your sobriety?

	No problem	Some problem	Big problem
1. I am around other people who are drinking.			
2. Someone who is important to me is still drinking.			
3. Family members disapprove of my not drinking.			
4. Friends disapprove of my not drinking.			
5. Other people feel uncomfortable because I am not drinking.			
6. People offer me a drink.			
7. I am embarrassed to tell other people that I am not drinking.			
8. Someone I live with is a drinker.			
9. Most of my close friends drink.			
10. I go to parties and celebrations where there is drinking.			
11. I try to help someone who drinks too much.			
12. I am around drinking at work or school.			
13. Someone I love drinks too much.			
14. People pressure me to have a drink.			
15. People give me a hard time for not drinking.			
16. Other:			

Miller, W.R., ed. COMBINE Monograph Series, Volume 1. Combined Behavioral Intervention Manual: A Clinical Research Guide for Therapists Treating People with Alcohol Abuse and Dependence. DHHS Publication N0. (NIH) 04-5288. Bethesda, MD: NIAAA, 2004.

Georgi Distefano, LCSW & Melinda Hohman, Ph.D.

PARADIGM II
Exercise 2

IDENTIFYING SOCIAL PRESSURE SITUATIONS AND COPING RESPONSES

Client Name: _____

Situations (Person, Places, etc.)	Date/Time
	Coping Strategies

Miller, W.R., ed. COMBINE Monograph Series, Volume 1. Combined Behavioral Intervention Manual: A Clinical Research Guide for Therapists Treating People with Alcohol Abuse and Dependence. DHHS Publication N0. (NIH) 04-5288. Bethesda, MD: NIAAA, 2004.

Georgi Distefano, LCSW & Melinda Hohman, Ph.D.

PARADIGM II
Exercise

Client Name: _____

LEARNING FROM COLLECTIVE WISDOM

Ask the client to select two individuals they met at AA (or other approved self-help) and pose the following questions. Individuals selected to respond must have a minimum of two years continuous recovery.

1. What was the most important change you made (aside from not using) that has made you successful with your recovery?

Person A – _____

Person B – _____

2. What suggestions would you have for a newcomer?

Person A – _____

Person B – _____

3. What do you have to watch out for? What could sabotage your recovery?

Person A – _____

Person B – _____

4. Additional question: _____

Person A – _____

Person B – _____

Georgi Distefano, LCSW & Melinda Hohman, Ph.D.

PARADIGM II
Exercise

Client Name: _____

OLD/NEW BEHAVIORS

Old Behaviors:
(During substance abuse)

1. _____
2. _____
3. _____
4. _____
5. _____
6. _____

New Behaviors:
(In abstinence/recovery)

1. _____
2. _____
3. _____
4. _____
5. _____
6. _____

The behavior changes I still want to make are:

1. _____
2. _____
3. _____
4. _____

Georgi Distefano, LCSW & Melinda Hohman, Ph.D.

PARADIGM II
Exercise

Client Name: _____

WHAT IS IN MY CONTROL?
Where would you put these examples?

- Whom I marry
- My work effort
- My partner decides he/she wants a divorce
- Which college degree to earn
- The amount of taxes I owe
- Who is elected president
- The boss's decisions
- The music my children like
- Drinking and driving
- Other's feelings
- Drinking or abstaining
- How I respond

SITUATIONS/ISSUES I CAN CONTROL

_____
_____
_____
_____
_____
_____

Client selects issue:
1. _____
2. _____
3. _____

SITUATIONS/ISSUES I CANNOT CONTROL

_____
_____
_____
_____
_____
_____

Client selects issue:
1. _____
2. _____
3. _____

How do you handle situations/issues not in your control?

Georgi Distefano, LCSW & Melinda Hohman, Ph.D.

PARADIGM II
Exercise

Client Name: _____

MONITORING BOTH SIDES OF THE STREET
SUBSTANCE ABUSE AND MENTAL HEALTH

1. The mental health issue I have is:
   _____
   _____

2. My goals are:
   _____
   _____

3. My warning signs/triggers for mental health problems are:
   _____
   _____

4. My action plan to avoid problems with mental health includes:
   _____
   _____

5. When I neglect to take care of my mental health needs, I can create the following problems on the other side of the street:
   ↓
   _____
   _____

1. The AOD substance(s) I have abused are:
   _____
   _____

2. My goals are:
   _____
   _____

3. My warning signs/triggers for AOD use are:
   _____
   _____

4. My action plan to avoid AOD use includes:
   _____
   _____

5. If I were to relapse (return to AOD use), I can create the following problems on the other side of the street:
   ↑
   _____
   _____

Georgi Distefano, LCSW & Melinda Hohman, Ph.D.

PARADIGM III EXERCISES

Clinical Goals and Interventions for Paradigm III
Paradigm Developmental Model

Paradigm Stage	Client's Issues/Motivators	Date	Counselor Interventions
Paradigm 3: Self Regulation ***Clinical Goals:*** • Embracing change • Exploration of ACA issues • Ability to self-correct • Engage in new health practices • Relapse prevention • Integrate alternative behaviors • Ability to self-regulate constantly ***Interventions:*** 1. How I Have Changed 2. Examination of Growth Zones Part I and II 3. Self Regulation Planning 4. Amends 5. ACA Old Behaviors Today 6. Building My Future **Paradigm 4: Transformation** ***Clinical Goals:*** • Giving back • Self-actualization • Resolve family/origin issues			

Client Name: _____ Cl #: _____ Counselor: _____

Georgi Distefano, LCSW & Melinda Hohman, Ph.D.

PARADIGM III
Exercise

Client Name: _____

HOW I HAVE CHANGED

1. Select adjectives to describe the negative aspects of your personality/behavior during your drinking/using period: (Circle all that apply).

Self-centered	Dishonest	Defensive
Preoccupied	Neglectful	Manipulative
Uncaring	Abusive	Scared
Self-involved	Argumentative	Ashamed
Depressed	Resistant	Anxious
Fearful	Aggressive	Negative
Unreliable	Reluctant	Unhappy
Thrill-seeking		

Other: _____

2. Select adjectives to describe yourself today: (Circle all that apply)

Caring	Responsible	Positive
Involved	Cooperative	Appreciative
Spiritual	Engaging	Grateful
Content	Assertive	Motivated
Steady	Proactive	Reliable

Other qualities I like best about myself are (describe): _____
_____

3. What do I do on a regular basis to maintain these qualities?:

1. _____
2. _____
3. _____

Georgi Distefano, LCSW & Melinda Hohman, Ph.D.

PARADIGM III
Exercise 1

Client Name: _____

GROWTH ZONE WORKSHEET
What's in your zones?

Part I

Name Activities/Issues/Responsibilities or Situation of Significance in Each Zone

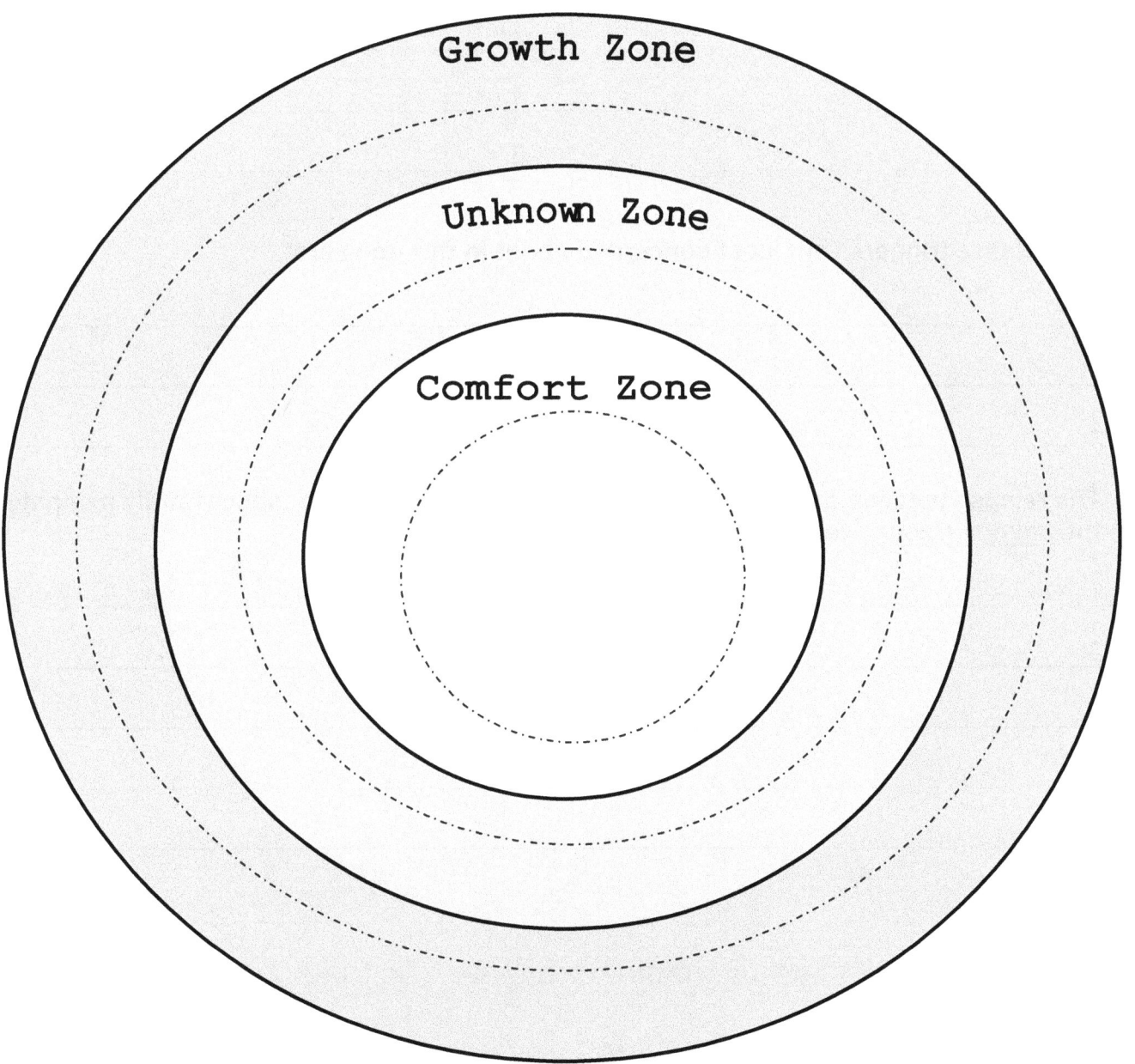

Georgi Distefano, LCSW & Melinda Hohman, Ph.D.

267

PARADIGM III
Exercise 2

Client Name: _____

UNKNOWN ZONE WORKSHEET

Activities/Issues/Responsibilities in my <u>unknown zone</u> are:

1. _____
2. _____
3. _____

Feelings/Emotions I experience in this zone are:

1. _____ 2. _____
3. _____ 4. _____
5. _____ 6. _____

The relapse triggers I am most concerned about in this zone are:

1. _____
2. _____
3. _____

The relapse prevention activities I commit to utilize to help me successfully navigate the <u>unknown zone</u> are:

1. _____
2. _____
3. _____
4. _____
5. _____

Georgi Distefano, LCSW & Melinda Hohman, Ph.D.

PARADIGM III
Exercise

Client Name: _____

SELF-REGULATION PLANNING

Areas in which I want to improve and self-regulate are: (Circle all that apply)

Finances	Leisure time	Physical activity
Parenting	Relationships	Meeting/Involvement
Housekeeping	Food/Nutrition	Spiritual development
Health care	Work commitments	Educational development
Living situation	Friendships	

Other: _____

Area #1: _____

My problems tend to be:

1. _____
2. _____

My commitments are:

1. _____
2. _____

In order to keep my commitments I will take the following actions:

1. _____
2. _____
3. _____
4. _____
5. _____
6. _____

Georgi Distefano, LCSW & Melinda Hohman, Ph.D.

I will review my progress in this area on: (date)_____

I have reviewed my progress and I am:

- ☐ Satisfied
- ☐ Somewhat satisfied
- ☐ Dissatisfied

If dissatisfied or somewhat satisfied, to improve this situation I will:

1. _____
2. _____

I will review my progress again on: (date)_____

Area #2: _____

My problems tend to be:

1. _____
2. _____

My commitments are:

1. _____
2. _____

In order to keep my commitments I will take the following actions:

1. _____
2. _____
3. _____
4. _____
5. _____
6. _____

Georgi Distefano, LCSW & Melinda Hohman, Ph.D.

I will review my progress in this area on: (date) _____

I have reviewed my progress and I am:
- ☐ Satisfied
- ☐ Somewhat satisfied
- ☐ Dissatisfied

If dissatisfied or somewhat satisfied, to improve this situation I will:

1. _____
2. _____

I will review my progress again on: (date) _____

PARADIGM III
Exercise

Client Name: _____

AMENDS

WHO: _____

WHY: _____

What have I learned from this experience?:

1. _____

2. _____

What will be different going forward?:

1. _____

2. _____

WHO: _____

WHY: _____

What have I learned from this experience?:

1. _____

2. _____

What will be different going forward?:

1. _____

2. _____

Georgi Distefano, LCSW & Melinda Hohman, Ph.D.

PARADIGM III
Exercise

Client Name: _____

ACA: OLD BEHAVIORS TODAY

I – These behaviors and beliefs helped me survive my childhood:

1. _____
2. _____
3. _____
4. _____
5. _____

II – How do the same behaviors and beliefs hurt me today?

1. _____
2. _____
3. _____
4. _____
5. _____

III – What changes can I make today with this awareness?

1. _____
2. _____
3. _____
4. _____
5. _____

IV – What behaviors/beliefs contribute to my growth?

1. _____
2. _____
3. _____
4. _____
5. _____

Georgi Distefano, LCSW & Melinda Hohman, Ph.D.

PARADIGM III
Exercise

Client Name: _____

BUILDING MY FUTURE

The following routines/rituals help to anchor my life:

1. _____
2. _____
3. _____
4. _____
5. _____
6. _____

These people help to support, enrich and stabilize my life:

1. _____
2. _____
3. _____
4. _____

I maintain my balance and sanity by engaging in the following activities and behaviors on a regular basis:

1. _____
2. _____
3. _____
4. _____
5. _____
6. _____

Georgi Distefano, LCSW & Melinda Hohman, Ph.D.

I am alert to my personal relapse warning signs:

1. _____
2. _____
3. _____
4. _____

Should I experience a relapse warning sign, I will initiate the following plan of action:

Sign/Plan of Action:
_____
_____
_____
_____

Sign/Plan of Action:
_____
_____
_____
_____

Looking forward, the next area I want to improve for myself is:
_____
_____
_____

EXERCISES FOR ANY PARADIGM

Clinical Goals and Interventions - at Any Stage
Paradigm Developmental Model

Client Name:_____ Cl #:_____ Counselor:_____

Paradigm Stage	Client's Issues/Motivators	Date	Counselor Interventions
AT ANY STAGE (Regardless the Paradigm the client is in) 1. Action Plan 2. Summary Session 3. Thinking about a referral 4. Medication non-compliance **Non-Compliance Interventions** 1. Resumed Drinking/Using 2. Missed Appointments/ Excessive Absences 3. Medication Non-Compliance 4. Referral Non-Compliance			

Georgi Distefano, LCSW & Melinda Hohman, Ph.D.

ANY PARADIGM
Exercise

ACTION PLAN

Client Name: _____

	SITUATION	GOALS	STEPS TO TAKE
FAMILY/RELATIONSHIPS			
RESENTMENTS/LOSSES			
FRIENDS/PEERS			
SELF INVENTORY / PERSONAL GROWTH			
RELAPSE PREVENTION / HIGH-RISK PREVENTION			

Georgi Distefano, LCSW & Melinda Hohman, Ph.D.

Paradigm III
Exercise   **Client Name:**_____

Date:	SUMMARY SESSION

☐ Review of the clinical dependency assessment.
☐ Review MAST/CAGE/AUDIT scores.
☐ Review of any insights gained by participant since the assessment.
☐ Review of participant's initial goals and motivators.
☐ Participant and counselor review Action Plan. Updated goals and motivators, high risk behaviors and warning signs as they relate to participant's history and chemical dependency assessment.
☐ Review of how participant has changed high risk behaviors.
☐ Participant's current reaction to self-help meetings and attendance.
☐ Review referrals and community resources offered. Accepted/Declined.
☐ Review of transition issues to next level of treatment, if any.
☐ Review of the PDMT scales and movement on the scale over the course of treatment.

Summary of discussion points and counselor recommendations.

_____
_____
_____
_____
_____
_____
_____
_____
_____
_____
_____
_____
_____
_____
_____
_____
_____
_____

Georgi Distefano, LCSW & Melinda Hohman, Ph.D.

ANY PARADIGM
Exercise

Client Name: _____

MEDICATION ISSUES

Utilize this exercise only if the client agrees it has value to them:

What are the medication(s) I have been prescribed? List:

_____
_____
_____
_____
_____
_____
_____
_____

I have stopped taking these medications because:

_____
_____
_____
_____
_____
_____
_____
_____
_____

What are the benefits of taking the medication as prescribed? What are the drawbacks?

PRO	CON

Georgi Distefano, LCSW & Melinda Hohman, Ph.D.

How does stopping this medication impact my ability to accomplish my goal regarding AOD use?

_____
_____
_____
_____
_____
_____

Would I benefit from a second professional opinion about the medication in question? Yes/No. Why?

_____
_____
_____
_____
_____
_____
_____
_____

Would I be open to trying a different medication Yes/No. Why?

_____
_____
_____
_____
_____
_____
_____
_____

In reflecting on the above questions – Do you feel you need or want to make any commitments to change at this time? What are they?

_____
_____
_____
_____
_____
_____
_____
_____

Georgi Distefano, LCSW & Melinda Hohman, Ph.D.

ANY PARADIGM
Exercise

THINKING ABOUT A REFERRAL

Client Name: _____

The referral I am considering is: _____

Reasons to Accept Referral	Reasons Against Referral

After the list is completed – rate each reason

1 – Not Very Important   2 – Important   3 – Very Important

Georgi Distefano, LCSW & Melinda Hohman, Ph.D.

LIST OF INTERVENTIONS BY PARADIGMS

	PARADIGM 1 — PROBLEM RECOGNITION	Date	Date	Date
1.	Providing Assessment Feedback			
2.	Motivators and Goals			
3.	Assessment: Loss/Grief/Anger/Resentment Family/Friends: Attitude/Support			
4.	Assessment: Identification of High-Risk Behaviors			
	Selecting Interventions			
5.	General MI Discussions. MI Discussion Using Change Talk Questionnaire. Additional Change-Talk questionnaire.			
6.	Consequence History / Looking Forward			
7.	Decisional Balance			
8.	Personal Values Card Sort			
9.	Discussion of Drinking Change - Personal Ruler			
10.	Mutual Support Group and AA - Reactions to AA			
11.	Identifying Craving/Urges and Triggers: Playgrounds, Playmates and Playthings			
12.	Determining Unmanageability			
	PARADIGM 2 — SELF-EXAMINATION – TAKING RESPONSIBILITY			
1.	Self-Examination and What is my Communication Style?			
2.	Change Plan Worksheet			
3.	What gets in the Way?			
4.	Revisiting my Goal and Motivators			
5.	My Cultural Influences			
6.	Trigger Response Plan			
7.	Urge Monitoring Card			
8.	Social Pressure Situations and Coping Responses. Exercise 1 & 2			
9.	Learning from Collective Wisdom			
10.	Old/New Behaviors			
11.	What is in my Control?			
12.	Monitoring Both Sides of the Street			
	PARADIGM 3 — SELF-REGULATION			
1.	How I Have Changed			
2.	Examination of Growth Zones - Part 1 and Part 2			
3.	Self-Regulation			
4.	Amends			
5.	ACA (Old) Behaviors Today			
6.	Building My Future			
	ANY PARADIGM INTERVENTIONS			
1.	Action Plan			
2.	Summary Session			
	NON-COMPLIANCE ISSUES			
1.	Medication Non-Compliance — SEE NON-COMPLIANCE SUGGESTED INTERVENTIONS LIST			
2.	Referrals Non-Compliance			

Georgi Distefano, LCSW & Melinda Hohman, Ph.D.

Georgi Distefano, LCSW & Melinda Hohman, Ph.D.

Published by Montezuma Publishing.

Please direct comments regarding this product to:

> Montezuma Publishing
> Aztec Shops Ltd.
> San Diego State University
> San Diego, California 92182-1701
> 619-594-7552

or email: *montezuma@aztecmail.com*

website: www.montezumapublishing.com

Production Credits
> Production mastering by: Lia Dearborn
> Quality control by: Jacob Kalmonson

This anthology contains copyrighted material requiring payment of royalties to the publisher of $5.00.

ISBN-10:   0-7442-4144-8
ISBN-13: 978-0-7442-4144-0

Copyright © 2017 by the author(s), Georgi DiStefano. The compilation, formatting, printing and binding of this work is the exclusive copyright of Montezuma Publishing and the author(s), Georgi DiStefano. All rights reserved. No part of this work may be reproduced, stored in a retrieval system, or transmitted in any form or by any means, including digital, except as may be expressly permitted by the applicable copyright statutes or with written permission of the Publisher or Author(s).

All copyrighted materials contained herein are reprinted with the express written permission of the original copyright holder. Acknowledgments and copyrights used by permission appear at the back of the book, which constitutes an extension of the copyright page. It is a violation of the law to reproduce these selections by any means whatsoever without the express written permission of the copyright holder(s).

Every effort has been made to trace all the copyright holders. But if any have been inadvertently overlooked, the publisher will be pleased to make the necessary arrangements at the first opportunity.

All copyrighted material reprinted with permission from the respective copyright holder. All rights reserved. Material may not be reproduced, in whole or in part, in any form whatsoever.

"Entire Text" from The Paradigm Developmental Model of Treatment with CD of Clinical Workbook, by Georgi DiStefano and Melinda Hohman, © 2010 San Diego State University Research Foundation.

Every effort has been made to trace all the copyright holders. But if any have been inadvertently overlooked, the publisher will be pleased to make the necessary arrangements at the first opportunity.

www.ingramcontent.com/pod-product-compliance
Lightning Source LLC
Chambersburg PA
CBHW081259170426
43198CB00017B/2844